# Clash

**Annika Sommer**
**SeventyEight**

# Chapter One: KickOff

The clock struck 9:00 PM, and the faint hum of a PlayStation booting up echoed in Omar's small living room. The coffee table was a battlefield of cola cans, half-eaten shawarma wraps, and a bowl of stale chips. Omar lounged on the couch, controller in hand, scrolling lazily through the game menu. His Madrid jersey clung snugly to his broad shoulders, its white fabric pristine as though it were a badge of honor. "You're late," he called out as the door creaked open. Youssef walked in, carrying a six-pack of soda and wearing an old, slightly faded Barcelona jersey. "Yeah, yeah," he muttered, kicking the door shut behind him. "Traffic was insane. It's like everyone in this city forgot how to drive all at once."

"Maybe they're all on their way to witness your inevitable defeat tonight," Omar quipped, not even looking up.

Youssef plopped down on the other side of the couch, throwing a pillow at Omar. "Big talk for someone who lost last time we played. What was it? Six to one?"

"Please," Omar said, dodging the pillow. "That was a fluke. Like Brexit. Everyone regretted it five minutes later."

Youssef grinned, cracking open a soda. "Brexit, huh? That's rich coming from you. Your team is basically the football equivalent of American imperialism—throwing money at every problem and hoping it works."

"Better than your club's strategy of begging Messi to come back while selling stadium seats just to pay the light bill," Omar shot back.

"Fair," Youssef admitted, leaning back with a chuckle. "But at least we're not selling souls to oil tycoons like City or PSG."

Omar picked up a shawarma wrap and pointed it at Youssef like a weapon. "Speaking of selling souls, did you see the news about the Saudis hosting the next World Cup?"

"Yeah," Youssef said, his grin fading. "They're turning football into a circus act. But honestly, the bigger betrayal is what the Arab leaders are doing to Palestine. Have you seen the footage of Gaza lately?" Omar sighed, setting the shawarma down. "It's a massacre. Every time I think we've hit rock bottom, the world finds a new way to disappoint me. And the so-called leaders— what a joke. Shaking hands with occupiers while their people are dying."

"They don't care," Youssef said bitterly, his voice low. "They're too busy chasing deals, hosting galas, and pretending to be progressive for the West. It's disgusting."

There was a moment of silence between them, broken only by the soft background music of the game. "You know," Omar said after a pause, "it's ironic. The same people who scream about 'values' and 'freedom' are the first to turn their backs on those who actually need help. And it's not just the Arab world. Look at Europe—what's happening there?"

"Ah, Europe," Youssef said, shaking his head. "The birthplace of democracy, now crawling with these so-called 'Christian nationalist' parties. Racists hiding behind religion. They talk about preserving culture, but all they're doing is sowing hatred."

Omar smirked humorlessly. "And don't forget America. The land of the free and the home of the brave—or should I say, the land of endless elections and the home of Donald Trump wannabes." Youssef burst out laughing. "Speaking of which, did you see the debate last week? The Republican guy—what's his name?—said the solution to climate change is planting trees. Like, we're burning fossil fuels at an industrial scale, but sure, a few saplings will fix it." Omar chuckled, shaking his head. "Honestly, I'm not even surprised anymore. This is the same country where half the population thinks vaccines are a government conspiracy."

Youssef leaned forward, grabbing a chip. "You know what it is? The world is stuck in this cycle of stupidity. Leaders focus on winning, not governing. Kind of like you, actually—playing for penalties instead of scoring actual goals."

Omar gasped in mock offense. "How dare you? I am the Benzema of FIFA—strategic, precise, and a certified winner."

"You're more like the Hazard of FIFA," Youssef shot back. "Overhyped and underperforming." They both laughed, the tension from their heavier conversation melting away.

"Alright," Omar said, hitting the start button. "Enough talk. Time to show you why Real Madrid is the greatest club in history."

Youssef grinned, his fingers tightening around the controller. "Bring it on, imperialist scum." The match began, the screen lighting up with the roar of a virtual stadium. As their players darted across the field, their conversation drifted again, jumping from war-torn Gaza to rising rents in their city, from the failure of politicians to the absurdity of modern memes.

But one thing remained constant: their laughter.

# Chapter Two: First Half

The TV blared with the sound of the game's kickoff whistle as Omar and Youssef leaned forward, controllers in hand. The tension in the room was palpable, not because of the virtual football match, but because both of them had too much pride to lose. "Alright, let's settle this once and for all," Omar said, squinting as he moved Vinícius Jr. down the left wing. "No excuses. No 'controller malfunction.' No 'this version feels weird.'"

Youssef smirked, his fingers flying across the buttons. "Relax, Benzema. You sound like one of those tech billionaires during a Congressional hearing—'This isn't my fault. It's the algorithm.'"

"Big talk for someone whose defense is already falling apart," Omar retorted as Vinícius cut inside, taking aim at the goal.

But Ter Stegen, Youssef's virtual goalkeeper, leaped into action, saving the shot spectacularly. "See that?" Youssef said, throwing a fist in the air. "That's German engineering at its finest. Your Brazilian wonder boy just got schooled."

Omar leaned back, groaning. "Oh, please. The only reason Ter Stegen's relevant is because Neuer keeps hogging the German starting spot. You're like that one guy who brags about owning a Tesla but drives it like a Prius."

Youssef grinned, intercepting a pass. "And you're like one of those crypto bros—spending big on talent, hyping it up, and then watching it all crash and burn when the season starts."

Omar snorted, his focus shifting to Benzema making a run. "Speaking of crashes, did you see that disaster in the GOP debate last week? Half the candidates couldn't even define climate change without googling it."

"Oh, I saw," Youssef replied, narrowing his eyes as he defended against another attack. "That one guy, what's-his-name—Ramaswamy? He said the solution to global warming was drilling more oil to boost the economy. I swear, they're running a simulation at this point."

"America," Omar said with mock reverence, pausing the game to make a substitution. "Where the cure for everything is either tax cuts or Jesus."

"Or guns," Youssef added. "Don't forget the guns. Nothing screams 'freedom' like arming your five-year-old."

They both laughed, the game resuming as the banter continued. Youssef's Dembele sprinted down the wing, dodging a clumsy tackle from Omar's Carvajal. "Speaking of disasters," Youssef said, taking a shot that narrowly missed the goal, "what's your take on Europe these days? Between the economy and those new nationalist parties, it's like watching Barça try to balance their books. Painful and embarrassing." Omar nodded, counter attacking with a swift pass to Modrić. "It's a mess. The 'Christian nationalist' types are basically rebranded fascists. And the economy? Inflation's so bad, I saw a meme the other day that said, 'A baguette in Paris now costs as much as a Neymar transfer clause.'"

Youssef burst out laughing, almost dropping his controller. "That's gold! But seriously, Europe is heading down a dark path. And the way they treat migrants? Disgraceful. It's like they've forgotten what it means to be human."

Omar's Benzema finally broke through Youssef's defense, scoring a stunning goal. He jumped off the couch, arms raised in victory. "GOAL! That's what happens when you focus on politics instead of defending."

Youssef groaned, slumping back into his seat. "Yeah, yeah, celebrate while you can. This is just the first half. I'm like the

French Revolution—biding my time before I decapitate your monarchy."

Omar laughed, shaking his head. "Please. You're more like the Arab Spring—starting strong but ending in chaos."

The room fell silent for a moment, the weight of Omar's words sinking in.

"You know," Youssef said quietly, "that's not even funny. Look at what's happening to Palestine right now. The Arab rulers are so busy cozying up to the West, they've left the Palestinians to fend for themselves." Omar sighed, setting his controller down. "Don't remind me. Every time I see the news, it feels like a punch to the gut. Entire families wiped out, children buried under rubble, and the world just shrugs." Youssef nodded, his gaze fixed on the screen. "And the leaders? They issue a statement, take a few photos, and then go back to shaking hands with the same people funding the occupation. It's disgusting."

"Disgusting doesn't even cover it," Omar replied, his voice tight with anger. "It's betrayal. Plain and simple. These so-called leaders are more interested in maintaining their own power than standing up for what's right."

The two sat in silence for a moment, the game temporarily forgotten.

Youssef finally broke the tension with a wry smile. "You know, this conversation feels like watching a VAR review—long, frustrating, and ultimately pointless." Omar laughed despite himself. "True. But at least VAR eventually gives a decision. The world? It just keeps repeating the same mistakes."

Youssef grinned, picking up his controller. "Alright, philosopher. Let's get back to the game. I still owe you a lesson in humility."

"Bring it on," Omar said, restarting the match. "But don't cry when Modrić teaches Gavi how to actually play midfield."

"Oh, you mean the same Modrić who'll probably be in a rocking chair by next season?"

"Better a rocking chair than being forced to retire early to balance the books. Isn't that right, Busquets?" The banter resumed, as sharp and ridiculous as ever, weaving between football, politics, and the absurdities of life. By halftime, the score was tied, and the stakes were higher than ever.

# Chapter Three: Halftime

The game paused at the halftime whistle, the score locked at 1-1. Omar leaned back into the couch, stretching his arms above his head as if he had just run the virtual field himself.

"You're lucky the referee didn't see that foul earlier," Omar said, pointing at the screen. "That tackle on Vinícius was criminal. Your defender should've been sent off."

Youssef scoffed, setting his controller down. "Criminal? Please. That was clean. If anything, your player dove like he's auditioning for a Bollywood movie." Omar laughed, reaching for a shawarma wrap from the coffee table. "Bollywood? More like an American political debate—full of drama and no substance. Speaking of which, have you seen the nonsense happening in the States lately?"

Youssef grabbed a can of soda, popping it open with a hiss. "Oh, you mean the 2024 elections? What a circus. It's like they've got a reality show running instead of a democracy."

"Exactly!" Omar said, leaning forward. "One guy's promising free healthcare, another one's vowing to bring back coal jobs, and then there's that lunatic claiming he'll solve global warming by...what was it again? Building more pipelines?"

Youssef nearly choked on his soda from laughing. "Pipeline guy! Yeah, I saw that. Honestly, I think the U.S. elections are just FIFA Ultimate Team for politicians. Everyone's buying power-ups, and the only ones losing are the fans."

Omar shook his head, chuckling. "And don't get me started on Europe. Did you see that viral clip of the far-right leader in Italy giving a speech about 'preserving Christian values'? It's like watching a villain monologue in a Marvel movie."

Youssef smirked, grabbing a chip. "Yeah, and then half the audience clapped. Europe's been so focused on saving money, they forgot to save their humanity."

"True," Omar said, chewing thoughtfully. "And it's not just Europe. The whole world feels off-balance. Like everyone's playing politics the way you play FIFA—random buttons and no strategy."

"Hey!" Youssef protested, throwing a pillow at him. "That's rich coming from the guy who spent the entire first half spamming through balls to Benzema. You're like Elon Musk—one idea, and you run it into the ground."

"Better than you, Mr. 'Pass it to Messi and hope for the best,'" Omar shot back, laughing. "But seriously, don't you feel like the world's leaders are all clueless? From the Middle East to Europe to America, it's the blind leading the blind."

Youssef nodded, his expression turning serious. "Yeah. Look at what's happening in Gaza. It's not just a crisis—it's a moral failure. The world watches, posts a hashtag, and then moves on like nothing happened."

"It's sickening," Omar agreed, his voice heavy. "And the Arab rulers? They've completely sold out. Hosting summits and signing deals while their people are dying. It's betrayal at the highest level." Youssef leaned back, staring at the ceiling. "Sometimes I wonder if we've all just accepted that the world is broken. Like, we rant, we tweet, we argue—but does anything actually change?"

Omar took a sip of his soda, nodding slowly. "It's like we're all in this endless cycle of outrage and apathy. One minute, everyone's protesting; the next, they're distracted by a new meme or a celebrity scandal."

"Speaking of memes," Youssef said, his face lighting up. "Did you see that one with the dog wearing a tie, saying, 'I have no idea what I'm doing'? That's every world leader right now."

Omar burst out laughing. "So true. And the worst part is, they all pretend to have everything under control. It's like watching you play defense—pure chaos disguised as strategy."

Youssef threw another pillow at him. "Keep talking, Mr. Penalty Merchant. I'm about to score the comeback of the century in the second half."

"Sure you are," Omar said, grinning. "But first, let's settle the real debate: pizza or shawarma for round two?"

Youssef thought for a moment, stroking his chin dramatically. "Pizza. But only if it's loaded with toppings. None of that minimalist, three-slices-of-cheese nonsense."

"Deal," Omar said, reaching for his phone to order. "But no pineapple. If you suggest pineapple, I'm kicking you out."

"Pineapple doesn't belong on pizza," Youssef declared solemnly. "That's the one thing we can agree on, unlike your ridiculous belief that Cristiano Ronaldo is better than Messi."

"Here we go again," Omar groaned. "Do you have to bring that up every time? It's not even a debate. CR7 is a machine, a leader, a goal scorer, a…."

"A PR stunt with legs," Youssef interrupted. "Messi's an artist. Watching him play is like...I don't know, watching Van Gogh paint."

"Van Gogh? Messi's more like a flashy street artist but overrated," Omar teased. "Ronaldo's the Michelangelo of football precision and perfection." Youssef rolled his eyes, leaning forward to grab another chip. "Fine. Let's settle this on the pitch. The winner of the second half gets bragging rights for eternity."

"Deal," Omar said, grinning. "But you're going down faster than your Wi-Fi connection during a storm." Youssef laughed, grabbing his controller. "Keep talking, Madridista. Let's see if your 'team of legends' can actually score a goal without diving for penalties."

The food arrived just as they were about to start the second half, forcing them to pause the game again. They both dug into the pizza, the conversation drifting from football to their own lives, their jobs, and their dreams.

"Do you ever feel like we're stuck?" Youssef asked suddenly, his tone more serious.

Omar raised an eyebrow. "Stuck how?"

"Like...we're just going through the motions," Youssef said, gesturing vaguely with a slice of pizza. "Work, bills, gaming nights like this. It's fun, but sometimes I wonder if we're missing something bigger." Omar thought for a moment, then shrugged. "Maybe. But who's got the energy to fix it? I can barely get out of bed in the morning without my coffee, let alone change the world."

Youssef chuckled, nodding. "Fair point. But still, wouldn't it be nice to leave a mark? To do something that matters?"

"We already are," Omar said, smirking. "We're making history tonight—by proving that Real Madrid is better than Barcelona."

Youssef rolled his eyes, laughing. "You're impossible."

"And you're predictable," Omar replied. "Now, let's finish this match before the pizza gets cold." With that, they resumed the game, the banter flowing as freely as the cola. The world outside might have been in chaos, but for now, in this small living room, all that mattered was the scoreboard.

# Chapter Four: Second Half

The second half began with a renewed sense of rivalry. Omar adjusted his controller, cracking his knuckles theatrically.

"This is it," Omar announced. "Time to show you why Real Madrid is the king of Europe."

Youssef rolled his eyes. "You've been saying that since kickoff. Yet here we are, tied. Typical Madridista—big talk, little action."

"You'll eat those words when Benzema scores," Omar retorted, his fingers moving deftly on the controller. "Benzema? That guy's practically sponsored by VAR. Every time he's in the box, it's like the referee's itching to gift him a penalty."

"And Messi?" Omar shot back. "He walks around the pitch like he's lost his glasses and can't find them."

"Walking? That's called reading the game," Youssef said smugly. "Something your team wouldn't understand. All you know is to cross and hope for the best." As the banter escalated, Youssef's virtual Messi picked up the ball near midfield, weaving through Omar's defenders like a needle through fabric.

"Look at that artistry!" Youssef cried triumphantly. "He's practically painting the Mona Lisa with his feet!"

"And here comes Casemiro to ruin the painting," Omar said, grinning as his defensive midfielder lunged in with a crunching tackle.

The ball ricocheted out of bounds. "Foul!" Youssef shouted. "That was an assault!"

"That was clean," Omar countered. "If this were the World Cup, Casemiro would be getting a medal for that."

Youssef groaned. "Typical Madrid logic. Bend the rules, then claim moral superiority. Honestly, you people are like world leaders—pretending to play fair while rigging the system."

Omar paused the game, giving him a mock-serious look. "Oh, so now we're dragging world politics into this? Fine. Let's talk about fairness. Like how the U.S. claims to be the champion of democracy while meddling in everyone else's elections."

Youssef raised an eyebrow. "Oh, you mean like how Real Madrid claims to develop players, but actually just buys them off other clubs?"

"Don't change the subject!" Omar said, laughing. "But okay, fine. Let's talk about that. What about your guy Messi skipping taxes in Spain? I guess the rules don't apply when you're the 'GOAT,' huh?"

"First of all," Youssef said, wagging a finger, "Messi paid those taxes. Secondly, that's rich coming from a fan of a team that gets bailed out by banks every other season."

"Oh, please," Omar scoffed. "That's called smart financing. Something Barcelona clearly doesn't understand, given your club's debt looks like the GDP of a small country."

Youssef laughed so hard he almost dropped his controller. "Smart financing? Is that what you call bribing referees? Because it seems to be working." They continued the game, the ball pinging back and forth as their banter reached new heights. "Speaking of corruption," Youssef said casually, "have you seen what's happening in Europe lately? All these far-right parties popping up like mushrooms after rain?"

Omar nodded grimly. "Yeah, it's scary. They're using the whole 'protect our culture' nonsense to rally people. Meanwhile, actual problems like healthcare and climate change get ignored."

"Exactly," Youssef said, his voice tinged with frustration. "It's like people forgot what happened the last time fascism got popular. Do we need another world war to remind everyone why it's a bad idea?"

Omar sighed. "And the worst part? They're not even subtle about it. They're openly racist, openly xenophobic, and people are still voting for them. It's like watching a train wreck in slow motion." Youssef shrugged. "What do you expect? Fear is a powerful tool. They blame immigrants for

everything—unemployment, crime, you name it. It's easier to point fingers than to fix the system."

"And then there's the Middle East," Omar added, his tone growing heavier. "Leaders signing deals with Israel while Gaza burns. It's like betrayal isn't even a strong enough word anymore."

Youssef clenched his jaw. "Don't even get me started. They're not leaders; they're businessmen. Selling out their people for a paycheck. And the rest of the world? They watch, they condemn, and then they go back to their Netflix shows."

"Yeah," Omar said bitterly. "Hashtags and hollow speeches. That's all we get. No action, no accountability. Just more death and destruction." The room fell silent for a moment, the weight of the conversation settling between them. "Maybe we're expecting too much," Youssef said finally. "Maybe the world's just...broken."

"Maybe," Omar agreed. "But I'd still like to think we can fix it. Even if it's just in small ways." Youssef gave him a wry smile. "Like beating you at FIFA? Because I'm about to score." And just like that, the tension broke. Youssef's Messi sprinted down the wing, cutting inside before unleashing a shot that soared past Omar's goalkeeper. "Goooaaaal!" Youssef shouted, leaping off the couch. "That's how it's done!"

"Lucky," Omar muttered, furiously mashing buttons as the replay played. "I'll get you back."

"Keep dreaming," Youssef said, sitting down with a smug grin. "You might win at debates, but on the pitch? You're out of your league."

The match continued, their laughter and trash talk filling the room once again. For all their complaints about the world, here in this moment, they found solace in each other's company—and in the game that had always brought them together.

# *Chapter Five: Extra Time*

As the final whistle of the regular match blew, the score stood tied. Omar tossed his controller onto the couch in mock frustration.

"Extra time it is," he said, stretching his arms. "Unlike your team, Youssef, I'm built for endurance." Youssef smirked. "Endurance? Coming from a guy who celebrated a 1-0 win against Getafe as if it were a Champions League final? Please."

"You wouldn't know real endurance if it hit you in the face. You guys spent an entire season passing the ball sideways and calling it tiki-taka. It's called attacking football, Youssef. Look it up."

The screen loaded for extra time as the two friends settled back into their seats. The room, once filled with the laughter of banter, was now charged with an unspoken tension.

"Speaking of endurance," Youssef said, his tone shifting slightly, "do you think anyone in Gaza has any left? With how things are going, I'm surprised anyone has the will to keep fighting."

Omar's smile faded. "It's not about will. It's about survival. They don't have a choice. If they stop fighting, they lose everything. That's what people like us sitting in comfort fail to understand."

"Oh, so now you're the voice of the oppressed?" Youssef said, raising an eyebrow. "You were just ranting about how Europe is falling apart. How's that different? Those far-right parties you were complaining about? They feed off the same kind of hopelessness."

"That's not the same thing, and you know it," Omar shot back, his hands gripping the controller tighter. "Europe has a choice. Gaza doesn't. They're trapped in a cage while the world looks the other way." Youssef sighed "And whose fault is that? Their so-called leaders? The same Arab rulers who'll sit down to tea with anyone offering a fat check? Or is it the people who just sit back and tweet hashtags?”

“Don’t act like it’s that simple!” Omar snapped, his voice rising. “You think every Palestinian wants to be a martyr? They’re just people, Youssef. People who want to live normal lives, but they’re forced into this nightmare because no one will help them.”
Youssef paused the game, turning to face Omar. “And what about here? What about the racism, the hate that’s growing in our own backyard? Or do you only care about injustice when it’s thousands of miles away?” Omar rolled his eyes. “Of course I care. But let’s not pretend it’s the same thing. Sure, racism is terrible, but at least here you can speak out against it without getting bombed to pieces.”

Youssef leaned back, crossing his arms. “Spoken like someone who doesn’t understand the roots of the problem. The hate we see here? It’s fueled by the same systems that oppress people over there. Colonialism, exploitation, it's all connected.”

“Oh, here we go,” Omar said sarcastically. “Blame colonialism for everything. Let’s ignore the fact that some of these problems are because people refuse to take responsibility for their own actions.”

“Responsibility?” Youssef repeated, his voice rising. “You mean like the responsibility Europe took when they started two world wars? Or the responsibility the U.S. shows by meddling in every other country’s politics?”

The match resumed, but their focus was clearly elsewhere. Omar’s Real Madrid players struggled to keep up with Youssef’s relentless Barcelona attacks, but neither of them cared much about the score anymore.

“You know what your problem is?” Omar said after a few moments of silence.

“Please, enlighten me,” Youssef replied, his tone dripping with sarcasm.

"You think everything is black and white," Omar said, gesturing with the controller. "Good versus evil. Oppressors versus oppressed. The world doesn't work that way, Youssef. It's all shades of gray." Youssef laughed bitterly. "Shades of gray? That's what people say when they don't want to pick a side. Neutrality is a luxury, Omar. One you can afford because you're not the one being bombed, jailed, or silenced."

"And you think shouting slogans makes you any better?" Omar retorted. "At least I'm honest about the fact that I can't change the world. You? You act like posting articles on social media is some kind of revolution." Youssef's face hardened. "At least I'm trying. What do you do, Omar? Sit on your couch and play FIFA while the world burns?"

"Don't you dare act like you're better than me," Omar snapped. "You're sitting on the same couch, playing the same game. Or did you forget?"

The room grew tense, the air thick with unspoken frustrations. On screen, the match was nearing its end, but neither of them seemed to care. Finally, Youssef spoke, his voice quieter but no less intense. "Maybe we're both hypocrites. But that doesn't mean we stop talking about it."

Omar sighed, his anger deflating. "You're right. It's just...hard, you know? Feeling like nothing you do matters."

"It's hard for everyone," Youssef said. "But that doesn't mean you give up. If we stop caring, then the people who actually want to make things worse win." For a moment, they sat in silence, the game forgotten. Then, as if on cue, Youssef's virtual Messi scored a dramatic goal in the dying seconds of extra time. "YES!" Youssef yelled, jumping up. "That's what I'm talking about!"

Omar groaned, burying his face in his hands. "Unbelievable. I let you distract me with your moral grandstanding."

"Excuses, excuses," Youssef said, grinning. "Now, let's see if you can survive the penalty shootout." As they prepared for the final showdown, the tension between them eased, replaced once again by the familiar rhythm of playful rivalry. Despite their differences, despite the weight of their conversation, they knew this night wasn't really about the game—or even their arguments.

It was about the bond they shared, one strong enough to weather their disagreements and keep them coming back to the same couch, night after night.

***Chapter Six: The Final Whistle*** **The penalty shootout began with the same intensity that had marked the rest of the match. The screen's stadium lights flickered as Omar's Courtois prepared to face Youssef's Messi in the first penalty attempt. "You do know Messi is overrated in penalties, right?" Omar said, breaking the silence.**

Youssef scoffed. "That's rich coming from a guy whose entire penalty record relies on Sergio Ramos and VAR." Messi lined up, ran, and shot—top corner. Goal. Youssef grinned smugly.

"Art. Pure art."

"Lucky," Omar muttered as he prepped Benzema for his shot.

The game on the screen was tense, but the energy in the room was heavier. Despite the playful trash talk, the conversations from earlier lingered. "Alright," Omar said after Benzema converted his penalty. "Let's settle this once and for all. You said neutrality is a luxury. Fine, I'll admit that. But what's your solution, Youssef? How do you expect people like us—two guys sitting in a living room, playing PlayStation to change the world?"

Youssef paused the game, leaning back against the couch. "It's not about fixing everything, Omar. It's about doing something. Anything. You can't just sit back and say, 'Oh, the world is too complicated, so I'll just opt out.' That's a cop-out."

"So you're saying I should what?" Omar asked, genuinely curious. "Protest? Write letters to politicians? Post on Instagram?"

"Yes," Youssef said, throwing his hands up. "All of that! It might not feel like much, but if enough people speak out, it can create a ripple effect. Look at history. Movements don't start with governments, they start with ordinary people."

Omar frowned, staring at the screen as Youssef's Lewandowski prepared for another penalty. "You know what history also shows? That people get crushed when they stand up. Revolutions get hijacked, leaders get corrupted, and nothing really changes." Lewandowski's shot went wide, and Omar smirked.

"Miss. Just like your argument," Omar said, trying to lighten the mood.

Youssef ignored him. "You sound like the people who justify not voting. 'Oh, my vote doesn't matter, so I won't bother.' Meanwhile, extremists and opportunists are voting in droves, shaping policies that affect everyone."

Omar shrugged. "It's not that I don't care. I just feel powerless. And honestly? Sometimes it feels like people like us arguing over these things is pointless. We're not the ones making decisions."

"And that's exactly what they want you to think," Youssef shot back. "That you're powerless. That you're too small to make a difference. It's the ultimate scam." The game resumed, but the dialogue grew more intense. "Fine," Omar said. "Let's talk specifics. Gaza. You keep talking about doing something. What can I realistically do to help people who are being bombed and blockaded half a world away?"

"You can amplify their voices," Youssef said passionately. "Share their stories, donate to credible organizations, and pressure your local representatives. It might not stop the bombs, but it shows solidarity. It shows that someone cares."

Omar rubbed his temples. "But is that enough? People have been doing that for decades, and the situation hasn't improved. If anything, it's gotten worse." Youssef's voice softened. "Maybe it's not about fixing everything, Omar. Maybe it's about not letting the world forget. Because the moment people stop caring, that's when all hope is truly lost." Omar nodded slowly, but his expression remained conflicted. "You make a good point. But it still feels...small. Like trying to put out a forest fire with a cup of water."

Youssef smiled faintly. "Better a cup of water than nothing at all."

As the penalty shootout neared its climax, the conversation shifted to other topics, but the tension lingered. They debated the rise of far-right politics in Europe, the consequences of climate inaction, and the growing polarization in their own society. "Do you think it's too late?" Omar asked at one point. "For us, for the world?"

Youssef hesitated before answering. "I don't know. But I don't think giving up is an option. If we stop trying, what's the point of anything?"

Omar nodded, his eyes fixed on the screen. The final penalty was his to take. Vinícius Jr. lined up the shot. "Miss this, and you owe me dinner next time," Youssef teased, trying to lighten the mood. Omar grinned. "Deal. But if I make it, you're admitting that Real Madrid is better than Barcelona."

"In your dreams," Youssef said, laughing. Vinícius ran up and struck the ball. It sailed past the virtual keeper and into the net. Omar threw his arms up in victory while Youssef groaned dramatically. "Unbelievable," Youssef muttered. "Typical Madridista, winning with luck."

"And typical Barcelonaista, always making excuses," Omar retorted, grinning.

They set their controllers down, the game finally over. But the discussions they'd had during the match lingered in the air, unresolved.

"You know," Youssef said after a pause, "we're never going to agree on everything."

"True," Omar admitted. "But maybe that's okay. As long as we keep talking."

Youssef smiled. "Talking, arguing, yelling at each other it's all part of the process."

Omar laughed. "So, same time next weekend? For the away game?"

"Absolutely," Youssef said. "But next time, we're ordering shawarma instead of pizza."

"Deal," Omar said, raising an imaginary toast. "To debates that never end."

"To debates that never end," Youssef echoed, clinking his water bottle against Omar's.

As the night drew to a close, the two friends cleaned up their gaming setup, their minds still buzzing with the weight of their discussions. They knew they hadn't solved anything that night, but they also knew that wasn't the point.

In a world full of noise and division, their friendship was a reminder that dialogue no matter how heated was the first step toward understanding.

The End